UNPLUG

RAISING KIDS IN A TECHNOLOGY ADDICTED WORLD

Lisa K. Strohman, J.D., Ph.D.
Melissa J. Westendorf, J.D., Ph.D.

ISBN: 978-1-4834-2954-0 (sc)
ISBN: 978-1-4834-2953-3 (e)

Library of Congress Control Number: 2015905959

Lulu Publishing Services rev. date: 7/6/2015

This book is dedicated to the countless parents, teachers, and young adults we have worked with through legal and emotional issues, personal tragedy and loss, and the simple yet painful reality of emotional and interpersonal strife caused by technology.

Contents

Introduction ix

      Who Should Read This Book xii

      Why *You* Should Read This Book xii

Chapter 1:   Technology 101 1

      Technology Addiction vs. Overuse 3

      The Slippery Slope of Technology 6

      Is it Possible to Underuse Technology? 7

      Who's Teaching Whom? 7

      The World Wide Web 8

      Technology Is Everywhere. Now What? 11

Chapter 2:   Technology and the Brain 13

      Structural Development 13

      Chemical Development 14

      Decision Centers and Structural Changes in the Brain 14

      Pleasure Centers and Chemistry in the Brain 18

Chapter 3:   Technology Use Continuum 23

      How do you know you need help? 23

Chapter 4:   How Too Much Technology Affects Kids' Behavior 26

      Behavioral Strategies 30

Chapter 5:   How Technology Overuse Manifests in
               Physical Symptoms 33
                   Physical Strategies 35

Chapter 6:   How Our Emotions Are Affected by Too
               Much Technology 39
                   Emotional Strategies 43

Chapter 7:   How Overuse of Technology Impacts our
               Interpersonal Relationships 45
                   Interpersonal Strategies 49

Chapter 8:   Tracking Technology Use 53
                   The Technology Use Log 54
                   Tracking Tips By Device 55
                   Analyzing your technology use logs 56

Chapter 9:   Setting Boundaries 58
                   Television 58
                   Gaming Systems 61
                   Computers 62
                   Phones 63
                   The Technology Usage Contract 63
                   Timers 65

Chapter 10: Overcoming Challenges 67
                   The Family Meeting 67
                   Lead by Example 69
                   Inform All Caregivers 70
                   What to Expect 71

Final Word 75
Acknowledgements 77
About the Authors 79
References 81

Introduction

There's no denying technology is an increasingly integral part of all our lives. People stay connected to work, family and friends almost constantly through smartphones, tablets and laptops. While there are benefits to living in a world with instant access to information and communication, there are also some serious consequences.

One of our biggest concerns is how technology use is affecting children. Seventy-five percent of teens have cellphones and average 4,000 sent and received text messages a month[1]. Moreover, studies show 97 percent of teens play computer games and 27 percent of those playing, play online with strangers. Twenty-three percent of children, ages eight to 18 report feeling "addicted" to video games.

Research clearly shows that technology overuse is detrimental to children and teens whose brains are still developing; it can lead to increased chances of developing ADHD, depression, apathy and anxiety. In its extremes, technology addiction can result in violence and fatalities.

TECHNOLOGY ADDICTION IN THE HEADLINES

"Addicted: Suicide Over Everquest?" CBS News October 2002: Shawn Woolley[2] committed suicide while sitting at his computer playing the game Everquest. His mother said she worried the 21-year-old was overly involved in the game when he quit his job, stopped seeing his family and stopped caring for himself.

"The Hold-'Em Holdup," NYTimes June 2006: Greg Hogan Jr.,[3] president of his sophomore class at Lehigh University, robs a bank to support his online gambling addiction.

"Pastor's Son Charged in Mother's Murder, Father's Shooting," Cleveland Plain Dealer October 2007: Daniel Petric[4] shot and killed his mother and tried to kill his father when they refused to let him play Halo 3, a video game rated M for mature, because of violence, blood and gore.

"Lakeland Girl Commits Suicide After 1 ½ Years of Being Bullied," The Ledger September 2013: Rebecca Sedwick,[5] a smart and pretty 12-year-old, was cyber bullied for the last time. After over a year of abuse, and despite parental intervention, she changed her name on a social media site to "That Dead Girl," and took her own life.

"Teen's texts encouraged friend to commit suicide," March 2015: Michelle Carter[6], 18, of Massachusetts was indicted for encouraging her friend Conrad Roy to go through with a long-discussed suicide plan. Upon further investigation, police not only found a text telling Roy to "get back in" after he expressed doubt in taking his life, they also came across 'hundreds' of texts between the two where Carter encouraged and guided Roy to take his own life.

The shocking headlines aren't to say that every child who overuses technology will resort to violence, but research supports a correlation between aggression and the use of violent video games. The stories outlined here indicate a growing problem that warrants parents' attention.

In our clinical practices, our communities and even in our own families, we see the negative impact of technology overuse. Children's behavior, physical health, emotional health and interpersonal relations are all falling victim to a world where technology is and must be a part of our everyday lives. The question is what can be done to change the situation, which is the heart of our message in "Unplug."

With technology intended to make life "easier," we see the work-family balance becoming more difficult. Like millions of others, we rely on technology to make our lives more manageable. Like many parents, we've used television, game systems and other electronics to occupy our kids while we make dinner, answer emails and return phone calls. As parents and practitioners, we understand the challenge of establishing technology boundaries for our children and ourselves. This book, written through the tears and laughter from parenting our own children in a technological age, is a work of passion.

We hope that our candid approach will help parents sort through the pros and cons of technology use and help you to better understand the effects technology use can have on children.

This book will teach you how the overuse of technology impacts your life and the people around you. It's important to understand why overuse occurs, what to do to prevent it and what to do if it's already taken hold of your family.

Who Should Read This Book

We wrote this book with parents in mind because, first and foremost, we are parents before psychologists. We also encourage everyone and anyone who cares for and works with children to read "Unplug" – teachers, grandparents, daycare providers, coaches, counselors, Sunday school teachers, aunts and uncles – everyone.

Why *You* Should Read This Book

In the real world, parents would never permit their children to go to a stranger's home alone and play games for hours. Yet, when children go online and connect with other users, that's exactly what happens. They engage with remotely located players, interact through social media sites and hold virtual conversations with people all over the world.

"Unplug" will help you recognize the potential for danger and provide tools for teaching and protecting children from the emotional and physical threats associated with technology use. It will also help you learn to set boundaries for technology use so your family can find balance between the virtual and real world.

As a companion to this book, we developed an online assessment tool, the Technology Use Continuum (TUC©), that breaks down the effects of technology into four main categories – Behavioral, Physical, Emotional and Interpersonal – which we explore in later chapters. The TUC assessment was scientifically designed to measure levels and areas of risk so parents can address issues before it is too late. To take the TUC assessment survey or to learn more, visit www.TechnologyWellnessCenter.com.

The stories we tell on the following pages do not represent actual patients, but they are based on stories we've learned of through our research and observed in our communities. Any similarities to real people are purely coincidental.

As you read these stories, we encourage you to ask yourselves if any of the scenarios fit your family. Do you see glimpses of overuse or addiction in your sons or daughters? Are you concerned that your child has a problem because they show some signs of overuse or addiction, but not others? This book was written to help you determine how to better manage raising children with technology, and to provide insight and practical tools for the challenges and choices our children are now facing.

Chapter 1

Technology 101

It might seem like we're stating the obvious, but let's start with the basics anyway. Simply put, we are defining technology as any electronic device that can be turned on or off.

- Computers
- Gaming devices
- Cellphones
- Televisions
- Digital music players
- Hand-held computers & tablets
- Children's interactive and "talking" toys
- DVD players
- Digital recorders

Is technology bad? No. We recognize that these devices solve and create problems. For instance, when you give your kids their own cellphones, it allows you to keep track of where they are at all times (as long as they keep them charged and don't lose them). At the same time, they are able to communicate with whomever they want, whenever they want, and say whatever they want without your knowledge. Gone are the days of knowing who is calling your child and vice versa. Essentially, the solution to one problem creates a different set of problems. With Internet connection at home on a steady increase since the late 1990s, children have more access to "friends" we don't know, which poses even greater challenges.

British anthropologist, Robin Dunbar,[7] said humans can maintain only 150 social relationships based on cognitive capacities. That's famously been dubbed the Dunbar Number. Dunbar's research demonstrates that humans do not have the capacity to know more than 150 individuals and it shows how each individual in that group relates to each other. Clearly, Dunbar's definition of friends is much different than Facebook's. Among 18 to 25-year-olds, Facebook users average more than 600 "friends."[8]

Today's children spend their lives connected. Marc Prensky, an expert in education and the effects of digital technology on learning, refers to them as "digital natives." He describes them as "the first generation to have spent their entire lives surrounded by and using computers, video games, digital music players, video cams, cellphones and all the other toys and tools of the digital age."

> *The US Census Bureau estimates that in 2011 78.1% of homes were connected to the Internet, in 2000, only 41.5% were.*[9]

Prensky estimates that by the time these digital natives reach college they will have spent less than 5,000 hours reading, more than 10,000 hours playing video games, and 20,000 hours watching television.[10] Add in the amount of time young people use technology to complete coursework, text friends, check social media and read email and you begin to understand just how much technology impacts their lives. Considering these numbers, it is a frightening reality.

Technology Addiction vs. Overuse

The term technology addiction is currently a non-medical term to describe observable behaviors. People often refer to addiction casually, "I am addicted to those chips" or "He's so addicted to that game." Addiction has two main components. The first is the behavior that causes a problem (i.e., playing video games); the second part relates to the persistence of the behavior. When a person continues to exhibit the behavior or to think about doing the behavior despite negative consequences, it can be considered an addictive disorder.

APA Puts Internet Gaming Disorder on 'Further Study' List

The Diagnostic Statistical Manual (DSM), the gold standard of psychology, just added the term "addictive disorders" in 2013 (though it never fully defines addiction). The inclusion of the "Substance-Related and Addictive Disorders" section merely defines what constitutes abuse or dependence and whether it is substance related (alcohol, marijuana) or non-substance related (gambling). During the massive rewriting of the DSM-5, members of the American Psychological Association had heated discussions about Internet Gaming Disorder as a diagnosis. Research was less clear in this area so Internet Gaming Disorder was placed in a section called "Conditions for Further Study," [11] which means additional research will be conducted to establish guidelines for an official diagnosis.

We would like to see the APA broaden the diagnosis of Internet Gaming Disorder to include more than gaming and Internet-based games. It should include iPad use, cellphone use and use of all interactive electronic devices. Eventually, we expect Internet addiction will be formally recognized as a disorder. When it is, it can be included in a patient's permanent medical record.

While we don't think it's appropriate to label children as addicts, we expect that the Diagnostic Statistical Manual will require us to so we are able treat and bill patients.

When working with children, we prefer to use the phrase "technology overuse" for two major reasons.

Reason 1: They are still growing and developing. Children have not yet developed critical thinking skills and labeling them with a disorder can have far-reaching, detrimental consequences. How, you ask? Let's compare a child "addicted" to technology to an adult with a substance or gambling addiction.

> **The adult:** He's diagnosed with a disorder when he loses his job or gets divorced because his actions (i.e. drug or alcohol use) have become unhealthy. The adult has the critical thinking skills to determine how he or she is going to respond. He can decide if he is going to accept the diagnosis and seek help to try to manage it, treat the diagnosis as a crutch to account for his behavior or ignore the diagnosis altogether and continue the addict behavior.

> **The child:** He's diagnosed with a disorder when he fails school, loses friends or gains weight because he is overly engrossed in technology. The child does not yet possess the critical thinking skills to manage a diagnosis. We believe that placing children in the same category as alcoholics and gambling addicts is irresponsible.

Reason 2: Others will treat a child labeled as an addict differently and possibly unfairly. As soon as the addict label is applied to a child, adults in his or her life are likely to view him or her as an addict and expect addict behaviors.

Ultimately, a formal, clinical diagnosis of Internet/computer/video game addiction would require extreme use with significant harmful consequences to qualify under healthcare guidelines. For an official diagnosis, the child would need to demonstrate neurological complications, psychological disturbances, and social problems that impact daily functioning. However, considering there is a subjective nature to this area and that there may be an incentive to obtain insurance funding for treatments and to justify services, it is very likely that a diagnosis would be recorded into the patient's permanent health record.

Should that clinical diagnosis and treatment be on a child's permanent health record ultimately placing him or her in a category with people battling gambling, alcohol, drug and other addictions? We don't believe it should.

Throughout the book, we will most often use the term "technology overuse," because we feel this more accurately describes the issues and behaviors that most children exhibit. And while their technology use may be a big contributor to their behavior issues, it doesn't technically qualify under an addiction definition.

While the formal diagnosis remains up for discussion, our colleagues are using Internet or technology addiction as a descriptor in their research. Although we prefer, technology overuse, we will also occasionally use the phrase "technology addiction," because it's what the general public, including parents, most frequently use to describe the behavior or issue, and to search online when seeking help.

The goal here is to protect children and provide parents with the help and guidance they need to ensure their children develop successfully.

The Slippery Slope of Technology

A persistent four-year-old who wants to watch "Frozen" for the fourth day in a row, or a 12-year-old who continuously asks to play games on the iPad needs to show more extreme behaviors to warrant serious concern that technology overuse or addiction is to blame. Is the child's behavior annoying? Yes. Are they addicted? Not necessarily.

The temptation for parents to give into demands is where the slippery slope begins. Sometimes it is harder to find compelling reasons to say no, and, let's face it, it's much easier to say yes. Technology is often the easy way out. When you plop your children in front of computers, gaming consoles, televisions and smart devices, you have fewer distractions. You can get ready for work, prepare dinner, enjoy some quiet time or squeeze in a couple hours of work-from-home time.

Raise your hand if you've justified doing this by sitting your kids in front of "educational" programming. Yeah, we have too.

> **Chelsea's Story: Too Much Technology Begets Bratty Behavior**
>
> After a few weeks of using technology as a babysitter, Chelsea's mom said her five-year-old no longer sought out her favorite pink crayon to draw with or dolls to play with. She only wanted to play computer games. Chelsea started arguing with her mother more often, becoming combative when her mom tried turning the electronics off. Rather than battle, Chelsea's mother found it was easier to give into her daughter's demands so she could complete her own household tasks.

Does this scenario sound familiar? It is common for children to want to use technology more and more once they begin. As difficult as it can be, it's our job as parents to impose limitations and set boundaries. Starting early with your children will set a foundation that can help prevent overuse.

Is it Possible to Underuse Technology?

Ryan's Story: Too Much of A Good Thing Begets Technology Deficit

Ryan's parents were always very strict about the time he spent online. Instead, they kept him and his brother busy playing on multiple sports teams and participating in outdoor activities. While most kids would watch TV or play on the computer after school, the brothers would play outside until dinnertime. Although both boys were active and healthy, when Ryan's mother met with his eighth-grade teachers, she found he was lagging behind his peers in his classes that required computer knowledge. The teachers pointed to Ryan's lack of computer literacy as a cause for concern regarding his readiness for high school.

Ryan's story demonstrates the importance of finding balance. We advise parents to err on the side of caution regarding the time children spend playing on the computer, especially when children are young. As they get into middle school and high school, technology will become a more prominent part of their academic and social lives. The goal is to help your children develop a level of competency that will allow them opportunities to succeed and learn how to find balance for an active, healthy lifestyle.

Who's Teaching Whom?

What parent has not asked a child for help programming some device, figuring out how to retrieve voicemails or set up a social media account? Most parents have come to rely on their kids to figure out how to use a new phone, computer or almost anything that requires an understanding of technology. In order to teach children balance, it's important to understand the world of technology our children are exposed to, which means it's necessary for parents to learn how to use it.

Parents who are unfamiliar with various technologies will have difficulty monitoring appropriate usage of technology, and, worse yet, set themselves up to be left out of their children's lives. Similarly, if you drastically restrict your children's technology use, like Ryan's parents, they may be excluded by their peers and fall behind academically.

The World Wide Web

There's no question that the ability to connect online 24/7 also has its benefits:

- The Internet provides access to volumes of information a school library could never hold.
- Students can connect with and learn about cultures all over the world instantaneously. (Those raised in the 1980s and earlier will remember having pen pals and the agony of waiting weeks for a reply.)
- Schools use social media to disseminate information on assignments and communicate with parents and students.
- Social media, when used properly, can provide up to the minute news updates, information on current trends and keep individuals separated by distance connected.

Children need to be familiar with all sorts of technology for their social, academic and future work lives. Therefore, raising a healthy, well-balanced child requires parents to be aware of the ever-evolving technologies and the dangers and benefits of its 24/7 access.

Vernon's Story: Living in Oblivion

Vernon, a 48-year-old father of two, received a new laptop for Christmas, despite not really wanting one. He liked to use the family computer for checking emails and occasionally looking things up on the Internet, but his wife was tired of listening to him fight their children to use the home computer. The kids were always online doing their homework – or so Vernon and his wife thought.

Vernon procrastinated setting up his new computer because he couldn't seem to find the instruction manual. Little did he know, it was already installed on the computer. All he had to do was plug the computer in, turn it on and follow the prompts. When he finally tried, he couldn't answer many of the prompts because he didn't understand the terminology.

Eventually, Vernon successfully set up the computer with his sons' help. However, despite all of this effort, he really only used his computer to play the basic solitaire game that came with the program bundle and to occasionally check his email.

Vernon will never know or understand what his children are doing online because he can't speak their language and doesn't understand their virtual culture.

Like many teenagers, his children spend far more time on social media than they do working on homework. Refusing to learn more about how things work left Vernon oblivious to what his kids were actually doing. Now, Vernon won't know if his children are at risk for technology overuse and its negative effects.

We are not asking parents to become tech experts or to set up profiles on every social media platform, but it is important for parents to know enough about technology to understand what their children are doing online. Learning what tools are out there and how they work makes it easier to monitor and regulate what children may be doing.

Hayley's Story: Strict Parents Stifle Social Life

Hayley was not permitted to have a cellphone until she was 18 years old because her parents heard horror stories of what happens when teenagers have cellphones. Her parents believed that because they got by without cellphones when they grew up in the 1980s, their daughter could do the same.

Hayley also wasn't allowed to have social media accounts. Her parents didn't use social media, and because they'd also heard alarming stories about the various social media platforms, they were unwilling to consider the potential benefits.

Haley was frequently left out of weekend outings with her friends because they'd made plans through texts and social media posts. They would frequently forget to call her home phone to let her know where they were going and she began feeling disconnected from her social group, which caused her to withdraw further. It wasn't long before she began exhibiting signs of depression.

In this case, Hayley's technology deficit caused similar problems to those seen in children who experience technology overuse, which we will explain in the next chapter.

Keeping kids from using a smartphone or social media site may seem like a good idea, but parents can't simply prevent technology overuse by completely restricting their children's access. In order to protect your kids from the dangers and teach them how to make good choices, parents need to understand more and fear less. We'll help you get there.

Technology Is Everywhere. Now What?

Schools now require students to use the Internet to complete assignments, conduct research, communicate with teachers and track their academic progress. Some schools even promote paper-free school days where all learning is delivered via technology. Today's children are growing up in an era where a lack of access to the Internet and computers will leave them unable to fulfill basic education requirements, and, worse, cause them to fall behind academically. While we stress that parents need to impose healthy limits on children's exposure to technology, they still need to encourage and help them develop their intellectual curiosity and understand exciting new technologies. Sounds conflicting? It comes down to setting limits and paying attention.

We can't tell you exactly how much time your family should spend online or what your technology use rules should be; that's your job. What we will do in the following chapter is provide tools to help you identify warning signs, define boundaries, correct problems and reinforce your family's guidelines.

Our hope as fellow parents, is that when you read "Unplug" you will walk away with a clearer understanding of the dangers, as well as some actual strategies you can apply to your own parenting practices.

To-do list:

- Don't "diagnose" your children as "technology addicts."
- Begin taking steps to prevent technology overuse.
- Stick to the technology use guidelines you set for your children and family.
- Don't give in, no matter how much they try to wear you down.
- Remember, what you do or don't do about your children's use can lead to a cycle of technology dependence and problems later.
- Recognize that technology plays an important role in today's society – it's not about using all or nothing.
- Strive for balance in your household.

Chapter 2

Technology and the Brain

If you have questions or concerns about how technology may impact your child's behavior, this is the chapter to read.

It is important to understand the biological consequences of technology use or overuse in order for parents to make an informed decision about "screen time." Currently, there are two significant areas that are being researched: the impact of technology on the structural development of the brain and the impact of technology on brain chemistry.

So, what is research telling us about our kids?

Structural Development

A study published in the European Journal of Radiology[12] found that teens who excessively play video or Internet games showed impairment of white matter fibers, which connect the brain regions that are involved in emotion generation and processing, executive attention, decision-making and cognitive control. Generally speaking, the study says that these teens have brains that are *structurally different* from their non-game playing peers. Children who experience this change in their brain matter might have developmental delays, difficulty processing information and problems maintaining relationships.

Chemical Development

Dopamine is the chemical released in our brains that mediates stress, promotes calmness, and generally manages mental well-being. The brain chemicals that control moods and feelings are chemically different in technology over-users than in those who are not excessively exposed to technology. As dopamine release is impacted and white matter in the brain begins to change structurally, your kids' moods and personalities are negatively impacted. We will address dopamine in more depth shortly.

Decision Centers and Structural Changes in the Brain

Everything we do has the ability to change the brain's structure. Even after initial brain development, the brain has the ability to repair, regenerate and develop new brain matter throughout adulthood thanks to what the medical field terms "plasticity."

A study published in The Journal of Neuroscience in 2003[13] analyzed the brains of musicians and found that gray matter volume in the areas musicians use most was highest in professional musicians, intermediate in amateur musicians, and lowest in non-musicians. String players have bulges on one side of the motor cortex because of fine motor control in one hand, whereas keyboard players have bulges on both sides of the motor cortex because piano playing requires fine control of *both* hands.

A 2006 study[14] showed that London taxi drivers had significantly larger hippocampus brain formations than bus drivers. This region of the brain specializes in spatial information for navigation, and taxi drivers do much more navigation than bus drivers who merely follow designated routes.[15]

So, if our brains are always evolving and changing, why should we be concerned about our kids and their technology use? Some may argue that if we can structurally improve and mold our brains as adults, we shouldn't be so worried about technology and its impact on children's brains. In fact, brain development of the prefrontal cortex doesn't fully develop until approximately age 25. This is the area responsible for judgment, impulse control, long-range planning and decision-making. If you have a teenager living at home who is impulsive, selfish and going through life without a plan, you probably just experienced an "ah-ha" moment.

The answer is that unlimited or unmonitored access to technology during critical periods of brain development can have significant negative effects. The research is too new to determine whether there are long-term consequences that cannot be repaired, but we are not willing to risk it.

Teenagers will choose to stay up all night gaming despite suffering the negative consequences of feeling too tired to pay attention in school. They impulsively send inappropriate text messages that include nude images or bullying remarks. These negative social, academic and physical consequences can and will arise because of the impulsive, poor decision-making associated with their not yet fully developed frontal lobe.

So what do brain-imaging studies tell us about kids? Technology overuse is modifying the brain in many areas during one of its most active developmental periods, and these modifications are contributing to a variety of serious issues.[16]

Difficulty Dealing with Social Conflict

The brain is designed to take in various social challenges and manage conflicts as part of normal development. These social challenges are essentially disappearing for our kids because they can go online to avoid the type of conflict we are intended to learn from.

More Susceptible to Addiction

Add excessive exposure to technology to an undeveloped pre-frontal lobe or, in other words, a brain that is already prone to immature decisions and impulsive behaviors and we find higher levels of affective disorders and addiction among teens.

Higher Rates of Depression

Adolescents are more depressed and anxious than ever. The number of adolescents reporting that they frequently feel anxious or depressed has doubled in the last 30 years, from 1 in 30 to 2 in 30 for boys and 1 in 10 to 2 in 10 for girls.[17]

An Increase in Teen Suicide

Even more disturbing is the information from the Centers for Disease Control and Prevention[18] which reported in 2011 that nearly one in six high school kids has considered suicide and one in 12 has made at least one attempt.

Risky Behaviors Become Riskier

The parts of the brain that are underdeveloped in heavy technology users are the areas used to stop a potentially risky behavior, also known as disinhibition. Disinhibition is great for gamers because the more daring you are in the game, the more likely you are to succeed. In the real world this can be dangerous – knowing when to show restraint helps keep us safe.

Kelsey and Brianne's Story:

Fourteen-year-old Kelsey accidently sent her friend Brianne a photo of herself partially nude. The message was supposed to go to Kelsey's online boyfriend, a cute 17-year-old surfer, she had never met in person because he lived in another state. Kelsey dismissed the misfired photo and said it wasn't her body. Brianne sensed something wasn't right, so she told her mom, who worked in law enforcement. Brianne's mother immediately alerted the police, and the police contacted Kelsey's parents. The police began investigating the situation by monitoring the exchanges between Kelsey and her surfer boyfriend. They uncovered a very serious online romance and a plan for a first meeting in the works. The "boyfriend" turned out to be a 40-year-old man posing as a teenager. When he showed up at Kelsey's high school to meet her, he was arrested. In his trunk, police found rope, duct tape, a shovel and lye.

Kelsey's parents never suspected a thing, and they didn't know anything about their daughter's online romance. While Kelsey was dedicating energy to her so-called relationship, she continued to keep up with her schoolwork, but had become a bit detached. Her parents noticed some changes, but attributed it to "normal" teen behavior.

So, how does this story connect to brain development? Good question. In the discussion earlier, we explained that individuals with undeveloped frontal lobes have a higher tendency to make impulsive decisions. While this has always been true, the Internet now exposes children to experiences and options they never had access to before. Now, the consequences they may face from making a poor decision to post information online can have frightening repercussions. We know that technology overuse can change how children's brains develop, we also know that it can negatively impact children's judgment.

We don't share Kelsey's story about the online boyfriend to suggest this will happen in all cases. We provide this example to emphasize how important it is to consider how vulnerable your children are. Their young brains lack the development that fosters good judgment, and potential structural deficits can be further affected by technology overuse, creating real threats to their safety.

Pleasure Centers and Chemistry in the Brain

Anyone who has kids knows how demanding they can be. A significant part of that can be attributed to the structural immaturity of their brains. Another major component is their brain chemistry. Research on brain chemistry is particularly interesting because it explains what makes people tick. Advancements in neuroscience allow scientists to see how a sip of caffeine or a single text message affects the brain.

Dopamine is the most widely researched neurotransmitter in addiction and brain chemistry science. The chemical is released as the brain anticipates rewards or when we achieve a goal. This "feel good" chemical drives people to continue engaging in pleasurable behaviors.

Every time your brain tells you to seek out your favorite meal or look for that one perfume scent that reminds you of a friend, it's because your brain is remembering a dopamine surge it experienced and wants it again. Older research indicated that dopamine was the neurotransmitter that allowed you to experience pleasure, but newer science is showing that dopamine is actually in charge of the seeking behavior itself and that opioids are what reward us with pleasure.

So why does it matter that dopamine is increasing your general level of arousal and goal-directed behavior? Because dopamine helps you stay focused and motivated to seek out new ideas. In terms of technology, once you start seeking – especially if you're getting instant results – it becomes harder to stop. Think about your smartphone and how often you check email, text messages, and social media. The gratification of seeing a new piece of information conditions your brain to want more. In the gaming industry, developers and designers are well aware of dopamine and use what they call a "compulsion loop" to keep people playing.

Programmers work to create a reward system for a player that is enough of a reward to get them to want to continue the game in order to earn the next reward. We could argue that this is no different than tobacco companies learning the science behind nicotine (also dopamine) and modifying their product in the same way. Dopamine forms the basis for most addictions.

Nicole's Story: Popular Game App Drains Bank Account

The first time she saw the game, she didn't understand why her friends were always talking about a popular game app. It was an easy game – so easy her 8-year-old sister could play it. She breezed through the first 20 levels quickly and found that the game was a great way to pass time between classes while waiting for the bus and at night before she fell asleep.

As the levels progressed, she noticed them becoming more challenging and more satisfyingly frustrating. She found online forums that posted "cheats," and she connected her debit card to her social media account so she could pay the small premiums to move forward, rather than wait for her popular social media friends to send her rewards. She loved spinning the daily prize wheel and even learned how to change the clock on her iPhone to trick the game into thinking 24 hours had passed so it would give her more rewards.

When Nicole's mom received a bank notice that her daughter's account was overdrawn she was shocked to see hundreds of debit charges ranging from $.99 to $19.99 to the social media platform.

The anticipation of reward is integral to something as basic as nourishment needed for survival. When dopamine is working, that's what drives you to continue to eat even after your body feels full.

It's what keeps you searching for something on the Internet even after you found the answer you were searching for. Your dopamine system says it wants more. The brain's inability to anticipate the next interaction is key to dopamine's effects, the Internet is the perfect reward system; you never know when or where the next reward will come. The amount and quality of the information is important in stimulating the dopamine system. Smaller bits of information leave you wanting more, which increases your anticipation. Text messages and other instant messages set you up to want to continue the process over and over as your dopaminergic process fuels the brain.

Dopamine-stimulating rewards are not new; it's what led to the evolution of humans. Learning how science and marketing get together and use dopamine rewards to incentivize you to continue consuming certain products will help you better understand why obesity rates among American adolescents (ages 12 to 19) have increased from 6.5 percent of the population in 1980 to 17.9 percent of the population in 2012, according to the Centers for Disease Control and Prevention.[19]

Intermittent Reinforcement

Here in lies the science behind intermittent reinforcement, marketing and human behavior. Behavioral researchers discovered that if you want to train an animal to do something, consistently rewarding that behavior is not the best tactic. In fact, the most effective training regime is one where you give the animal a reward at random intervals. Animals trained on an intermittent reinforcement schedule work harder for their rewards and continue the behavior long after the rewards for the behavior are removed.

It works even when the rewarding has stopped because the animal is now used to performing the behavior without receiving a reward. Humans operate the same way.

We can see this in action in Las Vegas. Gambling takes intermittent reinforcement to its highest level. When you randomly reward people for sticking money into a machine, they keep coming back, hoping for the next big pay out. Remember our discussion about dopamine earlier, now consider the role it plays in gambling. Dopamine creates the demand to place more money into the machine in anticipation of a huge payout.

Now let's apply the intermittent reward system to your home. When you randomly give in and allow your child to watch more TV, play another game or use the computer a little longer, you inadvertently establish the strongest and most effective reward system, the intermittent reinforcement system.

Now, let's look at how the intermittent reinforcement system applies to technology. It doesn't typically involve winning or losing money (which is what eventually stops most people from gambling), but it does involve random pay-offs. The interactions or messages from the smartphone, iPad, computer or gaming device is like Las Vegas for kids, but worse. Children are being rewarded randomly (every time they get a positive message, "like" or mention) and because they see no tangible negative consequences they become hooked.

Knowing what technology kids are using and how it works means there is actually hope and proof that parents can gain control with moderation and education. With kids, it is simply about providing them with consistent oversight, taking the intermittent reinforcement out of our parenting and being an active and present role model in their lives.

Knowing how the brain seeks out information and responds helps us understand how someone can become susceptible to technology overuse. Teaching kids about how dopamine affects their behavior needs to be part of the conversation, just like teaching them to be aware of the dangers of drugs and alcohol. Once children learn to recognize and override the compulsion-loop system they will gain more power and control. We also need to be aware of whether we are merely lecturing or if we are practicing what we preach. We will address this more in Chapter 10: Overcoming Challenges.

To-do list:

- Understand that technology overuse at a young age can permanently change a child's brain.
- When your child's actions don't make sense, remind yourself that the area of a child's brain responsible for good decision-making is not fully developed until age 25.
- Practice consistency.
- Teach your children about dopamine and how the brain anticipates rewards so they are better equipped to break an addict-like cycle.
- Do not attempt to diagnose when you see problems: seek a professional.

Chapter 3

Technology Use Continuum

We developed the TUC to help you assess whether your children and household might be headed toward trouble. The TUC system is a dynamic continuum meant for periodic use to evaluate the health and wellness of your household's relationship with technology. Your child's behavioral, physical, emotional and interpersonal risk from technology use will be evaluated, giving you a better idea of how to manage your family's technology time. You can access the TUC on our website at www. TechnologyWellnessCenter.com.

When taking the TUC, keep in mind it is normal for individuals to fluctuate between having balanced use and overuse. Results will change depending on the age of your children, their involvement in activities, and the pace of your work and family life.

How do you know you need help?

When a child has an injury, infection or other ailment, parents will typically take them to the pediatrician to find out what is wrong and what can be done to help. As an experienced parent, you become more adept at recognizing when you should seek help and when you should let an injury or illness run its course. The doctor will recommend treatment when injuries and illnesses are more serious. If the doctor prescribes the right solution and medication or treatment does what it should, life returns to normal. All is well once again.

When it comes to your child's mental health, it's more difficult to identify real problems because children go through so many emotional stages of ups and downs. Additionally, mental health treatments have a stigma attached to them, which discourages parents from taking their children to be treated.

We developed the Technology Use Continuum as an online test you can take in the privacy of your home to help determine when children are at risk and if families need to seek help for addressing issues related to technology overuse.

The TUC will give you an analysis of your child's risk for technology addiction based on the answers to questions covering four areas: behavioral, physical, emotional and interpersonal.

The questionnaire asks a variety of questions such as, "Does your child stop using technology when requested?" and you respond with a yes, no or sometimes. The responses are calculated to give you a risk rating ranging from none to severe. The higher the TUC score in each factor, the more at risk your child is for developing or already exhibiting unhealthy technology habits. Also, the higher the rating, the more likely your child's life is being negatively impacted by technology overuse. The four TUC factors identify areas of concern and allow you to utilize intervention tools to address the specific areas where your child struggles most.

We use these four factors as a basis for working with families in our practice.

Risk ratings are not set in stone. They can change based on the tactics parents use to help their children develop a healthy, balanced relationship with technology. We do not view the TUC scores as permanent scores but as a guide to tell you how your family is balancing its technology use and daily living. For example, your child may score higher on the TUC when they are in middle school, and because of your persistence, patience and intervention your child's score may move downward as he or she enters high school. In summary, the TUC is a dynamic tool that can help guide your family toward more healthy use of technology.

To-do list:

- Actively search for any signs your child might be suffering from technology overuse.
- Seek out a professional when you see a change that makes you concerned.
- Take the TUC bi-annually and make changes to your lifestyle based on your results.
- Remember: Your child's TUC results can, and likely will, change according to the strategies you use to combat technology use.
- When TUC results indicate risk, seek help to improve the situation.

Chapter 4

How Too Much Technology Affects Kids' Behavior

Technology use affects behavior, physical well-being, emotional health and interpersonal skills, the four areas assessed by the TUC. In the following chapters we will go into further detail on how these areas are specifically affected by technology use and how parents can manage their households in a way that minimizes the negative effects of too much screen time.

We can say with certainty that these behavioral factors are directly related to technology use. These behaviors are observable and can be impacted by the time and intensity children use technology, as well as their ability to stop using it.

Some behavioral factors include:

- Increased need to use technology
- Loss of interest in previously enjoyed hobbies
- Amount of time devoted to technology
- Impact on school performance (grades dropping)
- Effect on school attendance

- Increased conflict in the home

Behavioral markers of overuse or addiction will vary from one child to the next. While your child may not exhibit all the behavior markers, they may still be at risk.

Most children will use computers, gaming devices, cellphones and the Internet for extended periods of time if unrestricted. The same way they refuse to leave a birthday party, sit incessantly watching TV or play for hours with a favorite toy, they will persist in using technology, if allowed. What exacerbates this phenomenon is the slippery slope we talked about in Chapter 1. Many parents use devices as a type of babysitter to entertain the kids while they try to get things done, enjoy coffee with a friend, dinner with a spouse or any number of tasks. We've all done it, and we know it's unrealistic to expect parents to stop entirely. As long as parents keep the electronic time fillers to a minimum, the risks from overuse are less likely.

Behavioral concerns begin to arise when children demonstrate signs that they cannot let go of the technology. They refuse to turn it off and the more they play, the more they need to play. (Remember the lessons on dopamine in Chapter 2.) If their conversations revolve around technology and you rarely see them without it, then your child might be showing behavioral signs of overuse.

Theo's Story: Gaming Overuse Dashes Division-I Dreams

Theo was an A student. He was a high school junior who loved playing strategy games on the Internet. He had become an efficient player and progressed through levels quickly. In fact, he ranked among the world's best players. When he finally reached a level that was truly challenging, he spent most of his waking hours thinking about how to beat it so he could progress. Theo became consumed with researching how to beat the level, and began spending most of his weekends on the computer trying to advance.

As a junior, Theo was scheduled to take his college entrance examinations. To prepare he was supposed to attend practice SAT/ACT classes, but often skipped them in favor of more game time.

His parents were concerned about how much time he was spending in his room, but he convinced them he was preparing for his examinations and completing his homework. In lieu of studying, sleeping or socializing, Theo would play online until about 1 a.m. and wake up for school with only five hours of sleep. He began spending less and less time with his friends.

On the evening before his college entrance exam, Theo promised himself he would go to bed at a reasonable hour so he would be well rested for his test. Theo told himself he would play for only one hour and head to bed at 10 p.m., but the next time Theo looked at the clock it was 3 a.m. He worried if he went to sleep he would not wake up in time to make it to the test center, so he decided it was best to stay awake rather than try to sleep for a short period of time.

Although Theo felt awake during the exam and believed he scored well enough to earn a scholarship, he and his parents were shocked to see his scores in the lower fiftieth percentile.

Since Theo had always been a good student and his parents trusted him, they did not think it was necessary to set limits for his online game playing. Fortunately, they recognized the problem early enough to help their son and made arrangements so he could retake his college entrance exams.

Behavioral signs of too much technology:

- Losing track of time
- Spending less time with friends
- Inability to manage time
- Deceiving parents, teachers, friends
- Falling grades
- Lack of sleep, tiredness

Tasha's Story: Out of Sight, Out of Mind Actually Works

Tasha received a handheld gaming system from her grandparents for her twelfth birthday. She was excited because her friends had been talking about a particular game, and now Tasha could join the fun. The first week she played it whenever she was at home. Her parents granted her unrestricted access with a few limits; she could use her gaming device at home before bedtime as long as her homework was complete.

After her first week of playing, Tasha started to sneak her device into her bedroom so she could continue playing late at night. When her parents walked by her bedroom and found her gaming they confiscated the device for a week. The first day without the game was difficult for Tasha, and she accused her parents of being mean. On the second day, she complained that they were being too hard on her, but her parents did not relent. By day four, Tasha stopped pushing. Ten days later, she asked for it back, but promised not to break the rules again.

> Her parents acknowledged her for taking responsibility and recognizing the need to follow the rules. They also talked to her about self-regulating the time she spends using technology.
>
> While Tasha loved her new game and would play at every opportunity, she was able to disengage from her gaming system as long as her parents enforced the limits. She even went through a period of "out of sight, out of mind."

We do not believe technology overuse is defined by a child's desire to use technological devices or the frequency of use, it is based on how they respond to restrictions, and their ability to impose their own limits.

For instance, if you decide your daughter can only use the computer for 30 minutes in the morning, be sure you communicate the consequence for failing to follow the rule. If she exceeds her time limit she may lose her next allotted 30-minutes or face another consequence the two of you have agreed upon. The same rules could apply to cellphones. If you discover that your daughter is sneaking her cellphone into her room after her bedtime, then an appropriate consequence might be confiscating her cellphone for one day.

Behavioral Strategies

Behavioral problems due to technology overuse can cause children to lose interest in hobbies, drop out of extracurricular activities and start devoting excessive amounts of time to technology-driven activities. Technology overuse can negatively affect their performance at school and lead to increased conflict in the home.

Setting Expectations for Your Child

To help instill responsibility, we recommend you assign chores to your children, no matter their age. It should be an expectation that all family members contribute to the running of the household. You can make your own chore chart or you can download a customizable chore chart from our website, www.TechnologyWellnessCenter.com. Chore charts should clearly state which job duties are assigned to which child and include the frequency and the deadline for when a task should be complete. Another option some families choose for divvying out jobs is writing each chore on a small piece of paper and placing the chores in a bowl. Then each child picks his or her chore(s) at random and those are the chores he or she must complete for the week. Whichever method you choose, we believe it is very important to incorporate chores in to your child's life. It prepares them for independent living in college and teaches them the importance of contributing to a household.

A chart can also be a useful tool for teaching children to maintain good grooming habits. We are always amazed at the lack of hygiene and grooming that occurs when technology overuse becomes an issue. We have witnessed failure to brush teeth, take showers, and brush hair, not to mention a tendency to wear dirty clothes and have long, dirty fingernails. A grooming habit chart can help children be more aware of their personal hygiene and serve as a reminder for parents to monitor their children's grooming.

Establishing Guidelines for Technology Use

The most important thing you can do to prevent your children from over-using technology is set boundaries. Let's face it; children can sometimes act like professional beggars. When they want to get their way they can be relentless.

Who doesn't succumb to throwing a couple of coins in the proverbial cup to gain some much needed peace from time to time? When little Susie does not stop asking to use her handheld gaming device after bedtime and you are tired of repeatedly saying no you may eventually say, "Fine, but not for very long." This is the start of the slippery slope. When parents give in, it disrupts the boundaries and creates an ideal environment for behavioral issues to begin to develop. We know that we all make mistakes, so take this as a reminder to help keep slips to a minimum. Consistency, in the end, will make implementing boundaries easier for the entire family.

Also, keep in mind; rules aren't rules if there are no consequences.

To-do list:

- Set clear guidelines and expectations.
- Hold everyone accountable for abiding by the rules.
- Establish consequences if rules are broken.
- Reinforce good choices.

Chapter 5

How Technology Overuse Manifests in Physical Symptoms

The second area we address in the TUC is physical symptoms. Physical manifestations of a child's technology overuse can be the result of a number of other issues, but it's important to consider the impact when monitoring your child's overall health. If your child has difficulties in other areas – behavioral, emotional and interpersonal – pay close attention to their physical health as well. Physical symptoms may include:

- Unusual weight gain or loss
- Varying attention to hygiene
- Vision problems
- Dark circles under eyes
- Back issues
- Changes in sleep habits
- Poor eating habits or changes in appetite

Angela's Story: All-Night Texting Taxes Teen's Sleep

Angela was a 15-year-old high school freshman, cheerleader, babysitter and good student. At 13, her parents gave her a cellphone. When she started her parents upgraded her phone plan to include unlimited texting.

Angela's parents first noticed she had dark circles under her eyes and was drinking a lot of energy drinks. They then realized she was not consistently eating at mealtimes and she had difficulty getting out of bed in the morning. Angela dismissed her parents' concerns and said she was tired from late night studying, claimed she wasn't hungry because she ate after school and drank the energy drinks because they were nutritious.

Angela's parents also noticed that Angela frequently checked her phone and was never seen without it. She brought the phone to the dinner table, into the bathroom and kept it by her bedside.

When Angela's phone bill showed that she'd sent 4,500 text messages in one month, and at all hours, her mother knew it was time to take action. It became clear that her daughter's lack of sleep, poor eating habits and energy drink consumption was linked to her all-night texting.

Angela showed prominent physical symptoms of technology overuse. Fortunately, her parents noticed the changes in their daughter early on and checked her cellphone statement, where they were able to determine the root of the problem.

Emmanuel's Story: Parents Set Clear Rules For Tech Use

Emmanuel was an active, healthy 12-year-old child. He played guitar and loved to sing in the school choir. While not particularly athletic, he enjoyed karate and swimming. His family had standing movie nights on the weekends where they enjoyed sitting together eating pizza and watching a good family movie. He and his family also loved to play interactive video games, and although Emmanuel would have loved to continue playing the games after everyone went to bed, he knew that he would lose his game privileges if he argued about staying up late.

Emmanuel's parents taught him to be aware of what would happen if technology took over his life. When he sleeps less than 10 hours a night because he stays up late playing video games, he is crabby in the morning. When he watches his favorite cartoon channel on TV before school, he doesn't turn it off and he misses the bus.

His parents were aware of the consequences of technology overuse and they established clear rules and limits in their home to help Emmanuel learn technology management.

Emmanuel's family shows the importance of setting guidelines and teaching children how to live a balanced life with technology. His parents created awareness about the consequences of technology overuse, and they set clear rules on when it may be used in the home.

Physical Strategies

The physical signs of technology overuse are often easy to spot. A child overusing technology may lose or gain weight, become visibly sleep deprived or begin having vision problems. These physical changes often signal a serious problem that should not be overlooked.

Make sleep a priority

Sleep is one of the most important activities children do each day. Without sleep, they can become irritable, argumentative and impatient. Of course, going to school, engaging regularly in exercise or sports activities and socializing with friends are also very important, but none of these activities will result in success if a child is routinely sleep deprived.

Technology use immediately prior to bedtime can significantly interfere with a child's ability to fall asleep. The light emitted from the screen actually confuses the body's natural sleep cycle and affects melatonin levels.

Putting children to bed on a regular schedule helps ensure they get the sleep they need. To help make sure the sleep they are getting is a restful sleep, we suggest that technology use is complete at least a half-hour to an hour prior to bed time. We recommend unplugging devices by 9:00 p.m. if possible, and no later than 10:00 p.m. If you have teenagers, it will encourage them to get to bed earlier, especially when "there is nothing else to do." It is also a good rule for adults in the household. Adopting this strategy helps establish a sleep schedule in the home, which makes falling asleep and waking up easier on you and your children.

Avoiding Stimulants

It is also important to consider the amount caffeine and sugar children are consuming throughout the day. Caffeine is a seemingly innocuous ingredient in many of the drinks children are starting to consume by the time they hit middle and high school. The American Academy of Pediatrics recommends that adolescents (ages 13 to 18) consume no more than 100 mg of caffeine per day and children younger than 13 should not consume caffeine at all, as it has no nutritional value and acts as a stimulant. Our opinion is that kids shouldn't consume caffeine at all because it is mood altering and has no nutritional benefits. At the very least, we suggest you follow the advice of the medical community.

This is an even greater concern for children taking a psychotropic stimulant medication for Attention Deficit Disorder or Attention Deficit Hyperactivity Disorder. Children prescribed this type of medication should avoid consuming caffeinated beverages altogether. The interaction of the caffeine with the medication can cause cardiac problems and panic attacks.

Technology and Your Child's Vision

It is no surprise that research confirms that cases of myopia, or nearsightedness, have dramatically increased, likely due to computer use. Staring at a computer or mobile device requires focus. Most adults experience eyestrain from extensive screen time at work and at home. For children the extensive exposure to screens can create an even greater threat to their eyesight. Since children's fine motor skills for their eyes are not fully developed, their eye muscles are not physically mature enough for the stress caused by extended periods of screen time.

The American Optometric Association (AOA) indicates that children are at risk for computer vision syndrome if their computer use or screen time is not well monitored. Computer vision syndrome represents a group of eye and vision-related problems that result from prolonged computer use. In addition to eyestrain, the symptoms include blurred vision, headaches, dry eyes, neck and shoulder pain. To minimize your child's risk, the AOA recommends having their eyes checked regularly, limiting the time spent sitting at a computer and imposing frequent breaks from staring at a screen. The AOA also recommends adjusting the ergonomics of the computer workstation to fit children properly, eliminating or reducing computer screen glare, and matching the lighting levels in the room to the computer screen.

To-do list:

- Set clear guidelines and expectations.
- Establish consequences if arguments arise.
- Schedule regular family time.
- Encourage non-tech activities.
- Make sure everyone in your household gets enough sleep and encourage a tech-free bedtime routine.
- Consult a professional if you have any concerns.

Chapter 6

How Our Emotions Are Affected by Too Much Technology

The third area we evaluate in the TUC is emotional; emotional health is probably one of the more difficult areas to assess because of the normal waxing and waning of emotions that plague adolescence. Throw puberty in the mix and you have a brooding, complicated teenager full of angst for unknown reasons. As a result, it takes some detective work to try to parse out if emotions are part of normal adolescent development, if issues are tied to technology overuse or a result of some other event or underlying problem.

Emotional health factors include:

- Variation in mood or mood swings
- Depressive symptoms
- Anxiety
- Excessive anger
- A lack of demonstrated emotion
- Technology dependent mood states

After reading this list you can understand why it is tough to know if technology use is causing emotional problems. If a child exhibits these signs, don't try to diagnose their emotional health on your own. If you are concerned about your child's mental health, seek help from a professional.

To help recognize potential emotional health issues, we present two case studies where technology overuse clearly contributed to the children's well being.

Jimmy's Story: Happy Outgoing Scout Turns Into Moody Adolescent

Jimmy was in eighth grade and until middle school he was a happy, outgoing child. He was involved in sports and active in his local scout troop. However, when he entered middle school his disposition began to change for the worse. Without his parents' knowledge, he was actively involved in online multiplayer fantasy video games. He formed a legion with online friends and they competed against other legions around the world. As he became more involved with the game, he encouraged his real-life friends to join the game but they refused.

Jimmy lost interest in other activities and only wanted to talk about video games. His friends began to reject him and refer to him a nerd and a loser. He withdrew from his real-life friends and spent an increasing amount of time interacting with his online friends. He told his parents he wanted to quit his scouting troop and threw tantrums when his parents told him "no." Eventually they relented when he refused to participate in any of the programs.

Jimmy's parents noticed that he communicated less, ate less and appeared to be losing weight. He frequently refused to come to the table for dinner, claiming that he was not hungry and was tired of having to talk about his day.

Frustrated with his moodiness and isolation, Jimmy's parents unplug his computer. Jimmy was enraged and physically threatened his parents. Fearful of his behavior, his mother called the police when he started charging after his father.

The police officers removed Jimmy from the house, and took almost thirty minutes to calm him down. After speaking with his parents, the police agreed to allow Jimmy back in the home. Initially, Jimmy apologized to his father for his behavior and shortly after the police left his parents tried to talk to him about the incident. Jimmy became tearful and began yelling at his parents saying they did not understand him.

Overwhelmed and at a loss, the parents relented, allowing Jimmy access to his computer. Although his parents were uncomfortable with his online friendships, they were afraid he might have another violent or threatening outburst. This decision permitted Jimmy's continued outbursts and left Jimmy's parents feeling like they were failing him. It left Jimmy feeling out of control and remorseful after each episode.

Jimmy's case is an extreme example of what can happen when technology overuse leads to emotional problems. When most parents hear stories like this one, they think their child would never act out in this way. Unfortunately, in our line of work, we see it more than you can imagine.

In Jimmy's case, his parents recognized the changes in his behavior. They knew he was withdrawing and tried to set limits but when it was difficult to enforce, they relented instead of seeking the help. They mistakenly thought it was a phase that would pass, and did not take the proper steps to combat his technology overuse.

Emotional signs of technology overuse:

- Sullen and withdrawn
- Loss of interest in activities previously loved and enjoyed
- Alienation from friends/peers
- Temper tantrums, outbursts of anger and/or threats

Taylor's Story: Social Media Jeopardizes Social Life

Taylor was popular at school and had a number of close friends. When she started spending more time on her computer and smartphone, she began making friends online through social media. Her parents noticed she was spending more time at home in her room and less time socializing with her friends from school. She also began participating less in the recreational activities she normally enjoyed, like softball and swim team. Taylor appeared tired, withdrawn and unhappy.

Recognizing the changes, Taylor's parents held a family meeting where they told Taylor she had to participate in extracurricular activities in order to be allowed phone and computer time. They realized they also had to make modifications in their approach to technology to set an example. They set up guidelines restricting the entire family from technology at bedtime, and insisted on spending quality time at the dinner table together. They even established a weekly game night. Although Taylor initially resisted, her parents' example and her time spent with friends at her extracurricular activities helped her back into her old routine. She ultimately spent less time connecting with friends online.

In this case, Taylor's parents intervened before Taylor's behavior caused more serious emotional issues. They connected her changes in behavior and apparent unhappiness to her technology use, and they were able to successfully impose limits. By addressing the situation early and taking action, Taylor's parents helped her re-connect with her friends and family, which resulted in a happier household.

While these scenarios are simplified examples, stories like Jimmy's and Taylor's happen every day. If a teen's growing dependence on technology goes unnoticed or ignored, it will only become worse.

Emotional Strategies

Despite the hundreds of friends they are connected to on social media and the constant online interaction, research confirms that children today are more anxious, isolated, and lonely than any previous generation. Some researchers hypothesize that the over-scheduling of children coupled with electronic communication has crippled children's ability to be alone. In turn, an inability to cope with being alone lends itself to overusing technology and so it becomes a vicious cycle.

A strong relationship between parents and children is one of the most important factors in preventing technology-related emotional issues. In the following section we outline recommendations for activities and actions that help encourage children to share their feelings. These opportunities for discussion can help foster a child's emotional health.

Family Night

As we write this section we can already hear the groaning from adolescents (and some parents) about family night. It might take a bit of convincing to have your teenagers participate at first, but it is a wonderful way to stay connected with children. We recommend starting family night when your children are young so that it is already an accepted family practice, and hopefully a celebrated tradition long before your children reach adolescence.

The purpose of structured family time is to become more connected with your children and to provide them the opportunity to discuss important issues with you. It may take weeks or months before everyone in the family is "all in," but give it time and patience and soon everyone will look forward to these family events. Time can be spent playing games, doing something together outdoors, going to a sporting event or simply enjoying a meal together. Remember, family nights should be technology free; that means for Mom and Dad too.

Purposeful Daily Contact

It is extremely important that parents have face-to-face connection with their children every day, despite the craziness of their schedules. When a child returns home from school or outside activities, establish the practice of spending five to 10 minutes talking. Teach them to come in and find you to touch base. The same rule should hold true for parents when returning home. Go to them and chat about their day or what is happening that evening. These informal communications keep children connected to the family unit.

To-do list:

- Set clear guidelines and expectations.
- Watch carefully for changes in your child's demeanor.
- Encourage children to stay involved with their hobbies.
- Encourage children to stay in touch with their real-life friends.

Chapter 7

How Overuse of Technology Impacts our Interpersonal Relationships

The final area we address in the TUC is interpersonal relationships. Online, a child who has hundreds of friends and followers on social networking sites might seem like the popular kid with connections to people all over the world; however, a Princeton study[20] suggests the opposite. The authors found that heavy users of online communications and games experience increased loneliness and depression. The research also suggests that violent games contribute to increased aggressiveness, decreased sensitivity to others' suffering and an inability to distinguish real life from fantasy.

The most powerful impact technology overuse has is on interpersonal relationships. Trouble with interpersonal skills is a common problem seen in patients and is repeatedly brought into therapy.

Interpersonal skills may deteriorate during childhood and adolescence if children are not given the opportunity to develop and practice these skills with others. Children learn how to interact with others, monitor reactions from peers and alter their behavior from their social experiences. Feedback from face-to-face engagement largely comes in the form of nonverbal cues (facial expressions, posture). In the online world children do not have those cues to help them determine which of their actions are productive (leads to more friendships and genuine connections) or unproductive (which leads difficulty making friends and connecting with others).

Chuck's Story: Mom Dismisses Moodiness as Teen Angst

Chuck was a 17-year-old who never had a large group of friends; he had one best friend with whom he spent most of his time. He was always talkative with his family and enjoyed attending family functions. He conversed most often with adult family members, and most were impressed with his intellect.

When a falling out with his best friend left him without any close friends, Chuck spent an increasing amount of time in chat rooms and playing online fantasy games. He spent money purchasing various characters in the game, and started lying to his parents about why he needed money. When his parents cut him off and demanded he get a part-time job, he began sneaking his father's credit card to make purchases. He knew his father rarely looked at his credit card statements and thought he could get away with making several small purchases.

After receiving a call from the school, Chuck's mother discovered he had not attended classes in over a week. When she confronted Chuck, he claimed he had been feeling ill and thought it was best to stay home and recuperate. While she doubted his story, she realized that she spent so much time away from home that past week and had not seen her son much. Her own guilt about her absence and his excuses led her to conclude Chuck was just experiencing "senioritis." In truth, Chuck spent the week playing online games and was not concerned about school.

As Chuck got more involved in gaming he lost interest in spending time with his family. They had to coax him into joining them for dinner at home. He refused to go out with them to dinner and when he did join them, he rarely spoke.

This example demonstrates how an introverted, but fairly normal adolescent with good interpersonal skills can change how he interacts with others when technology overuse takes hold. Technology becomes the center of the child's social world and their interpersonal skills begin to suffer. As they become more involved in living life online, feedback for their interpersonal skill development is almost absent; if a situation like Chuck's continues, it can have a long-term impact on their ability to build social connections and meaningful relationships.

Common interpersonal relationship problems include:

- Poor communication skills
- Focus on online friends versus offline friends
- Disintegration of friendships
- Inability to disengage from technology
- Withdrawal from family
- Increased time spent alone
- Social awkwardness

Tracy's Story: Online Bullies and Balancing Friends

Tracy was a 16-year-old hockey player who came from a large family. She had six brothers and two sisters and often got lost in the controlled chaos of her family's busy schedule. She loved hockey and spent time with her team on and off the ice. The team frequently traveled for tournaments, and she spent most of her time on the bus chatting with her teammates and their parents. Most of her teammates' parents enjoyed speaking with Tracy and found her to be a well-adjusted, mature adolescent.

When hockey season ended, Tracy began spending more time talking with her friends via text and social media to remain connected. She became hooked on an online game she played with her friends. She even met new friends through the game, and thought most of them seemed pretty cool. After a month of playing, she realized some of her online friends were intensely involved in the game. She enjoyed the strategy and camaraderie, but didn't take it as seriously.

When the next hockey season rolled around, she told her online friends she wouldn't be around as much. Some of them tried to persuade her to remain connected to the game. One player became angry with her and even tried to bully her into continuing her involvement in the game. Tracy was upset and turned to her parents for advice. Her parents did not limit Tracy's Internet use but they did stress the importance of face-to-face relationships and staying involved in real-world activities. She agreed with their advice and remained active with her hockey team.

In this case, Tracy was involved in sports and possessed good interpersonal skills. She made friends from her various interests and these friendships changed during various time of the year due to where she spent her time.

Despite her interest in online gaming, and the pressure she encountered from online friends, Tracy was able to stay engaged with reality and maintain her interpersonal relationships with real-life friends. Tracy's case shows how strong interpersonal skills gained through family involvement and being part of a team provides children with the strength and self-confidence to make healthy choices and resist bullying. It also points to the importance of parental input in helping children prioritize and make decisions.

Interpersonal Strategies

Interpersonal strategies focus on helping children who have lost or failed to develop important social skills due to the isolation caused by their technology use. Redeveloping these skills is one of the fundamental components of returning them to the world around them rather than allowing them to remain lost in the fantasy world of technology. Taking the opportunity to engage children in conversations and social interactions as often as possible is valuable. The goal is to use strategies to assist children through the trials and errors of interpersonal development and to provide them with opportunities to learn or relearn to interact with others.

Use Technology to Your Advantage

Through much of our book we've talked about the pitfalls and risks of technology use. Now, shifting gears, we are going to focus on why you should use technology.

We all know technology is here to stay, and it would be tough to do a majority of our daily tasks if we didn't use it. Part of finding balance and teaching children how to have a healthy, balanced relationship with technology, requires parents to embrace it. With limits, of course.

With the steady stream of new technological developments, apps, devices and social media platforms kids are adopting, how do parents stay on top of it all? While we understand that it may not always be possible, it is imperative that parents learn about the programs and devices their children are using in school and at home and begin using them too.

For example, if you are a parent of teens, we encourage communicating with them through text. We are not telling you to text them to come down for dinner or to carry on in depth conversations, but send an occasional message during the day to see how they are doing, use it to check in and tell them you love them. Keeping up on the communication tools they use shows that you are not "stuck in the dark ages," and more importantly, it keeps the lines of communication open. It also reminds children that you are willing to work with them in this ever-evolving age of technology. This is a communication technique we encourage our clients to practice and the results are consistently positive. Both children and parents feel happier and more connected.

The Open Texting Experiment

This is a strategy that your child will dislike so immensely that they may even threaten to disown you; however, this exercise is so enlightening that it is worth the fight. Find a large writing surface, such as a big piece of cardboard, chalkboard, or poster board and then tape the paper to a wall in a public area of your house, (e.g., kitchen, family room, etc.). Next, choose one of your child's text conversations and tell the child the two of you are going to write the conversation on small strips of construction paper. Your child's texts should be written on one color of paper and their friend's texts can be written on another color of paper. Promise your child that you will not judge or criticize what is written in the texts, (e.g., profane language, sexual talk, etc.). Have your child write down their texts and you write down the friend's texts. Then, one by one tape the texts to the large board in the order the conversation developed. Try to pick a texting conversation that includes inappropriate language or comments you do not think your child would have said in person.

After taping these texts to the board, provide your child with time to make any comments about the conversation. Ask if the conversation would have been the same if they were face-to-face with the person or if they would want to change any of their comments now. After the child provides you with their thoughts, take the opportunity to provide your own constructive feedback about the conversation. Point out the other person's perspective or other issues you feel are important. It is vital that throughout the exercise you do not become judgmental and you keep an open mind. Remember, as adolescents we all talked in ways that our parents would have disapproved of. The difference now is these private conversations are being broadcasted over texts, tweets and other instant messaging services that become public and permanent. Use this exercise as a tool to help your child develop their interpersonal skills and understand the consequences their words may have on others.

To further encourage your child to participate in this activity, agree to post some of your own texting conversations. In fact, posting an electronic argument between you and your child might be a great way to discuss interpersonal skills (e.g., I should not have said this, or this is what I meant, etc.). If your child absolutely refuses to do this exercise then take this opportunity to discuss the fact that all texts are in the public domain and can be discovered by others. Their refusal to participate in this exercise can serve as a good catalyst for discussion.

To-do list:

- Set clear guidelines and expectations.
- Encourage extra-curricular activities.

- Empower children to make decisions.
- Keep lines of communication open.
- Facilitate activities that connect children with peers and provide opportunities to create bonds.

Chapter 8

Tracking Technology Use

This part of the book will allow you to use all of the knowledge you've gained up to this point and put it into action.

We begin by urging you to track your family's technology use for one week with the Technology Use Log (see below). Review and analyze the information you uncover and use it to begin to set guidelines and expectations that will help build better habits and practices for your family. The log will track how much time everyone in your household uses computers, cellphones, gaming consoles, television and other technologies.

Everyone? Yes, that includes parents.

We want parents to be aware of their own use of technology and the example they are setting for their children.

Have your kids ever complained that you text too much? Do you frequently answer work phone calls during dinner or family gatherings? Do you constantly check your cellphone for emails while out with the family?

If you hold yourself accountable first, and you are open and honest with your children, you will serve as a strong role model for them.

Technology overuse is a family problem because everyone is impacted. Gathering information about the entire family will help you implement the strategies you'll learn in chapters nine and ten.

The Technology Use Log

You can download our Technology Use Log from our website (TechnologyWellnessCenter.com) or you can create your own. Be sure to include:

- User name
- Date
- Time started
- Device used
- Activity (played game, scheduled a meeting, answered email, etc.)

If you are unable to monitor screen time, there are excellent programs available (we have many listed on our website) that can help with tracking computer use. These tools allow you to fully analyze and keep documentation of your children's computer usage.

To get started, track one weekday and one weekend day. Pick a weekday that best represents a typical day. For example, if your child is involved in sports on Monday nights but every other night of the week is spent at home on the computer, then selecting a Monday night is not the best night to track his or her use.

After that first step, try tracking an entire week.

Here is just a sample of what you should try to log:

Technology Type	Time	Total Minutes	Purpose

Tracking Tips By Device

- **Computer:** You'll find a list of tracking resources for members on our website, or you can search "parental control software" online.
- **Cellphone/smartphone:** Look at your most recent cell phone bill to learn more about your child's usage. Contact your provider and ask about parental control plans. For example, Verizon offers a FamilyBase plan for a small monthly fee, which gives detailed reports to parents about their children's phone, text and Internet usage.
- **Gaming:** Set a timer when your child is playing games online and make sure the gaming console is in the living room or other shared space where you can monitor their playing time.
- **Tablets:** Tablets that have an independent Internet connection can be equipped with the same parental controls as cellphones. You can also monitor how much time they are spending online by reading reports created by your service provider. For tablets that

operate off Wi-Fi, set a timer when your child is using the device and monitor them closely.

- **Television:** Use the parental controls; most televisions have these to make sure your children are watching appropriate programming. You can also set timers to ensure the television will turn off after the agreed amount of time has passed.

Analyzing your technology use logs

Once you collect your "data," add a column called "Frivolous, Fun and Fundamental."

- **Frivolous:** Items you identify as completely unnecessary, such as excessive time playing games or watching TV. These are items you will eliminate when you set boundaries.
- **Fun:** These items you identify as acceptable uses of your and your family's time. You will allow them to be used in moderation, within limits you set.
- **Fundamental:** These are must-have technology interactions. Online banking, paying bills and homework are examples of fundamental tasks online.

To-do list:

- Set a good example for your children by not overusing technology during family time.
- Track your family's technology use accurately.
- Get a clear snapshot of your family's technology use by tracking the days that most closely match a typical day in your household.
- Determine time limits for your children based on their technology use.

- Identify technology use as fundamental, fun or frivolous and unnecessary.
- Remember, you are in charge of determining the optimal amount of technology time for your family.

Chapter 9

Setting Boundaries

The guidelines presented in the following chapters are our recommendations based on research and our years of experience counseling patients. While we hope you will take these suggestions into consideration, we also encourage you to adapt them to fit your family's lifestyle. They will serve as a foundation to moderate your family's technology use. Whether the goal is to prevent future problems or to correct an issue your family is currently experiencing, setting healthy boundaries is the first step to raising a technology healthy family.

We encourage you to use the information you gathered in the previous chapters to set boundaries, and make adjustments as needed. Determine what works for your family and what doesn't.

Television

Research[21] indicates that most children are drawn to television long before they enter school. Some reports indicate that two-thirds of infants and toddlers watch TV an average of three hours a day. This number increases to nearly four hours a day by the age of eight. Once video games and

Internet use are factored in, the average eight year old is spending as much as six hours a day using technology or staring at a screen.

The American Academy of Pediatrics (AAP) recommends no television for children under the age of two. For our purposes, we apply this rule to all screen-based technology since the first two years of life are such a critical time for brain development. For children older than two the recommendation is no more than one to two hours of quality programming a day.

TV watching and technology use can impede valuable development activities like exploring, playing and interacting with parents and others. These functions are vital to learning and healthy physical and social development. When children are not using time for play and social interaction, a variety of issues are likely to develop.

To help curb usage, televisions should never be located in a child's room. One study[22] estimates that nearly 70 percent of kids eight to 18 have televisions in their bedrooms. While it is no surprise, studies show that children who have televisions in their bedrooms sleep less than the average child and watch more hours of television.

In addition to monitoring time, parents also need to monitor programming content. Most television shows display a rating in the upper right-hand corner of the screen for the first 15 seconds of airing, but not all TV channels offer the rating system. We recommend that you watch programs and research video games to ensure the general content and messaging fits with your family's values. IMBD and www.TVGuidelines.org are two great resources to find information on the content of television programs. You can also use parental controls through your cable company to block certain channels or programs that might air inappropriate content.

How to Interpret TV Ratings

Ratings Directed Toward Children

TV-Y – These programs are appropriate for all ages and are not expected to frighten or upset young children as they are specifically designed for viewers between the ages of two and six.

TV-Y7 – These programs are typically not appropriate for children under the age of seven as they feature fantasy that young children may not have the developmental skills to understand. These "make-believe" plotlines are more likely to frighten young children and should be avoided.

Ratings Directed Toward a General Audience

TV-G – These programs, though not specifically geared toward children, would be considered appropriate for all ages by most parents. They do not contain excessive violence, expletives or sexual references.

TV-PG – These programs have the potential to include some violence, some suggestive or sexual material and occasional strong language. They are likely not appropriate for young children to watch unattended, but are acceptable for older children.

TV-14 – Parents are cautioned to not allow children under 14-years-old to view these programs without supervision. These programs might include overtly sexual situations, inappropriate dialogue, indecent language or graphic violence.

*Ratings from the Federal Communications Commission (FCC)

Gaming Systems

Gaming systems are integrated with Internet connections and, if activated, they permit users to interact with other users all over the world. This means the afternoon online player in a foreign country becomes your child's all-night companion. This situation can be particularly dangerous when you realize how naïve kids can be. They can connect into worlds with fantasy play, allowing them seemingly unlimited powers. Your children can also play online unknowingly with sexual predators who are patiently and slowly gaining their trust. These predators watch and wait for children to lose themselves in the gaming world. Even when there is not a threat of a sexual predator, children allowed to engage in excessive or unmonitored video gaming become more susceptible to detaching from the real world.

How to Interpret Game Ratings

EC (Early Childhood) – These programs are developed for young children.

E (Everyone) – These programs are considered appropriate for players of all ages. They might feature fantasy elements unsuitable for young children, some inappropriate language or mild violence.

E10+ (Everyone 10+) – These programs are not suitable for children under the age of 10. They might include elements of fantasy, mild violence and inappropriate language. They may also include suggestive themes.

Teen (Teen) – These programs are appropriate for teens age 13 and older. These games might include fantasy, somewhat graphic violence and inappropriate language as well as crude humor and simulated gambling.

Mature (Mature) – These games are only suitable for players age 17 and older. They potentially include more graphic violence, sexual content and explicit language.

AO (Adults Only) – These programs are for adults older than the age of 18. They might feature intense and drawn-out violent scenes, graphic sexual content and explicit language. These games might also involve gambling with real currency.

RP (Rating Pending) – These programs expect, but have not yet received a rating from the Entertainment Software Rating Board.

*Ratings from the Entertainment Software Rating Board (ESRB)

Computers

Computers should also never be located in a child's bedroom. This allows the virtual "candy store" of information into your child's sleep zone. It's extremely unlikely you would permit your child to have cases of candy bars stored in his or her room to access whenever they would like. You would also not want your child walking into the home of strangers alone without telling you where he or she is. You have to treat the computer and Internet similarly. While the Internet can be fun and a great source of information, there are also many risks associated with it, when left unmonitored. Computers should be housed in areas where you can observe how they are being used and time limits and age-appropriate guidelines or rules can be imposed. The American Academy of Pediatrics recommends no more than two hours of computer time per day stating, "Children and teens should engage with entertainment media for no more than one or two hours per day, and that should be high-quality content. It is important for kids to spend time on outdoor play, reading, hobbies and using their imaginations in free play."[23]

This recommendation takes into consideration the physical, developmental and emotional consequences of too much screen time.

Phones

Phones, especially those equipped with Internet access, can be one of the biggest distractions for children. Providing a child with a smartphone can lead to less sleep and excessive usage. We recommend never allowing a child access to a cellphone with Internet connection in their room – especially at night. When given the freedom, children often use phones to send inappropriate content or play video games without adult supervision. Monitoring your child's phone usage, watching how much time they spend on their phone and setting clear rules for what your child can and can't do on their phone are the first steps toward effectively setting boundaries. We recommend not providing a phone to children who are in elementary school as they are too immature to deal with many of the responsibilities and challenges that come along with this privilege. Waiting until high school would be ideal, however some parents find this a difficult task when their preteen is incessantly begging them for a phone. If you decide that middle school is the right time to allow this privilege, be conscientious and have a contract in place with your teen. Implement as many of the parental restrictions as you can and review monitoring programs that can help you ensure there is no bullying, illegal transfers of pictures, etc. We have some suggestions for monitoring tools on our website (www. TechnologyWellnessCenter.com).

The Technology Usage Contract

Setting boundaries can be a challenge, especially when it comes to cellphone use. Implementing a clear set of guidelines from the beginning can help prevent issues later. One method or tool that can be effective is a usage contract.

A Technology Usage Contract looks like this:

> [Your child's name] agrees to not use his/her cellphone between the hours of 10 p.m. and 7 a.m. If [child's name] uses their cellphone during those prohibited times he/she will turn his/her cellphone in to [parent/adult] for one/ two/three days.

You and your child can determine the specific consequences for using the cellphone or other technologies during the prohibited time. The purpose of this contract is to establish a collaborative effort in developing the boundaries and guidelines for technology use in your home.

Neal's Story:

Neal's family established a technology use contract that stated if Neal had three or more cellphone violations within a week, he would be prohibited from going out with his friends for two full weekends.

It did not take long for him to violate the provisions. His parents informed him that he broke the contract and he was grounded. That Saturday, Neal proceeded to ignore his parents and invite a small group of friends over. When his parents reprimanded him, he insisted he was following the rules because he did not go out to spend time with friends.

How would you handle that situation? Neal's parents conceded and allowed his friends to stay. Later they added a clause to the technology use agreement so it wouldn't happen again.

Expect that children and adolescents will be crafty and that they will find loopholes. When you draft your contract, ask someone else to read it and try to find loopholes.

A sample Technology Use Contract can be found and downloaded from our website (www.TechnologyWellnessCenter.com).

Timers

Let's be real, time escapes when using social media, the Internet and computers in general. Have you ever started researching something on the Internet (or shopped for shoes) only to discover 90 minutes had passed and you still hadn't found the answer or the shoes? Your children have experienced the same scenario.

A simple tool to help limit time spent online is a timer. Place an egg timer or small digital timer next to the device in use. Set it to remind your child when he or she needs to end his or her technology time. This timing should not include "fundamental" technology time (see Chapter 8), but during homework tasks you should consider checking up on them to make sure they are not using the opportunity to sneak onto other sites.

Some parental monitoring programs will send alerts to you when the computer is being used, and allow you to turn off the computer remotely. There are also great programs that allow parents to limit children's access to websites.

Some devices come with built-in timers, or you can download apps that allow you to set usage limits and a password-lock to shut down the device when time expires. Check your manufacturer's website and app store for additional tools.

Our online Resource Center for our members is available at www. TechnologyWellnessCenter.com.

To-do list:

Recommendations for boundary setting

Television

- No TV in bedroom
- Use parental controls with passwords
- Set time limits
- Clearly set rating limit

Video Games

- No computer/video games in bedroom
- Use parental controls with passwords
- Set time limits
- Clearly set rating limit

Computers

- No computers in bedrooms
- Use parental controls with passwords
- Set time limits
- Clearly set rating limit

Phones

- No phones during class or other extra curricular activities
- Keep phone out of bedroom at night
- Monitor billing statements
- Use parental controls with passwords
- Set timers and use limits

Chapter 10

Overcoming Challenges

We wouldn't provide you with all these great tools and suggestions, and not prepare you for the challenges you may face. We understand how hard it is to be consistent when maintaining a busy lifestyle. Making it a priority to remain aware of your family's technology use and to consistently enforce boundaries, will help prevent technology overuse.

The Family Meeting

Once you have completed a weekly log and the TUC assessment, you will have a clearer picture of your family's technology use habits and risk levels. The next step we recommend is holding a family meeting (dragging your children kicking and screaming if you have to) to share the information you have learned. Simply making your family aware of their behavior and the risks associated will hopefully be enough to get them to agree to cut back on their technology use.

If you find yourself in this situation, then we offer you our congratulations on your insight and ability to use awareness of the issue to make the appropriate changes in your household. However, it is more likely that if you have family members that overuse technology, they aren't going to give it up easily. Whatever the situation is, we recommend that all families establish some basic guidelines to help establish a healthy balance of technology use. Coming together as a family and agreeing on a plan will help keep the household on track.

Include your children's input when setting the new guidelines. Doing so will give them some power in the process and help them become more invested. Ask them what they think is a reasonable punishment if they violate the rules of technology use. While some children will not provide you with a reasonable response, you might be surprised at how insightful and fair some of their recommendations are. If they have assisted you in determining the punishment, then when it comes time for implementation (and it will be necessary at some point), you can remind them that they helped establish the consequences.

The conversation may become easier if every one has a chance to write out what they most want from the meeting and what they would like to accomplish. If your kids are too young for this step you may have a conversation more like this:

Parent: "We are planning as a family to learn how to balance our technology use, just like learning to eat a balanced meal to keep us healthy. If you have too many cookies and not enough healthy foods we will get sick and be unhealthy. Technology is similar in that too much can make us unhealthy and we want our family to be healthy and make good choices. What are some examples of technology we have in our home?"

Child: "Television and the computer are technology."

Parent: "Great! You are right. What about our cellphones, gaming device, and our iPads?"

Child: "Oh yeah, I forgot about those."

Parent: "So let's figure out what we need to do to balance our technology use with other things. What kinds of things can we do that aren't technology related?"

Child: "We could go for a walk, or play a game maybe?"

...

As you can see from this sample dialogue, parents can talk to their kids about how they define technology use (in a way younger children understand) and also open up a dialogue that will engage children to help determine alternatives that they would enjoy doing, before discussing the limits and consequences.

As you go through the process of implementing solutions to technology overuse, your children will challenge and test you. When it comes to technology use there are many ways kids test the boundaries parents establish that, quite frankly, you can't always control. The best thing parents can do is stay informed and remain committed to creating a healthy, balanced household. Starting early in your children's life teaches them to be open and honest so they will be more likely to talk about threats and problems when they arise.

Lead by Example

Gandhi said it best, "You must be the change you wish to see in the world." Children are sponges soaking up everything around them, so it is important for parents to serve as the best role model possible.

Many people were outraged when professional basketball player Charles Barkley said, "I'm not a role model. Just because I dunk a basketball doesn't mean I should raise your kids."

At the time, the media took hold of his statement and crucified him for being naïve and selfish. Today, we somewhat agree with Charles and hope that parents understand his underlying message. The responsibility of raising children ultimately falls on the shoulders of parents. Parents are a child's primary role model and most important influence. Parents are the first ones children watch, and look to day in and day out to determine their sense of value and meaning in the world. Therefore, parents must lead by example and not just rule by command. More often than not, children do as their parents do, not as they say.

What does that mean for parents? It means making hard decisions when you are tired after a long day at work. It means you must remain strong and be consistent with your rules, even when it is easier to just give in rather than fight yet another battle. It means that when you get home from work or greet your children after school, you must stop trying to multi-task, answer emails, text friends or call colleagues and take a moment or more to engage in a meaningful conversation with your kids. Parents need to focus more on providing children with a good example of how to treat their friends and loved ones. Kids are smart, and they are watching their parents to learn what's right and wrong.

Inform All Caregivers

We've all heard the phrase "it takes a village to raise a child," and TUC strategies work best when you enlist the help of your village. That means teachers, grandparents, aunts and uncles, babysitters, older siblings, fellow parents, coaches and all other adults in your child's life.

What are grandparents for if not to spoil your kids and make them feel special? While we understand this is part of most family dynamics, it is important that grandparents and other relatives and caregivers are enforcing the rules you have set for your children. Go over your technology overuse prevention plan with your parents, your spouse's parents and other relatives or caregivers who play important roles in your children's lives.

Teachers and school faculty members will also be instrumental in preventing technology overuse. Schools have become more available to parents by permitting online access to homework progress and test completion. We recommend you take advantage of these resources. We also encourage you to develop a relationship with your children's teachers and guidance counselor so you are always aware of your children's standing in school. Let your children know that you are forming these relationships and will be checking up on their academic progress.

In our practices, we found that one of the most common behavioral consequences of technology overuse is the decline in academic performance. We have worked with children who are extremely bright and can pass tests with ease, yet suffer academically due to an issue with technology use.

What to Expect

The Extinction Burst

We couldn't in good conscience provide all of this information and encourage you to remain steadfast through this process without warning you about the potential for the technology use to get worse—at least in the beginning.

The nagging, tantrums, and indignant looks always emerge when you try to change a behavior, such as excessive cellphone use. It is tough to let go thanks to the dopamine triggers from the rewards and positive reinforcements from texts, posts, and instant messages. Your children have been conditioned to receive these technological rewards and, almost without thinking, will continue to try. This is called an extinction burst. Fortunately, it is usually short lived. Unfortunately, the burst can be extreme. Oftentimes this extinction burst breaks the will of parents who aren't prepared. Have faith that with consistency and appropriate boundaries you will break the habit and the demands. We encourage you to stay strong and seek out support from friends and family. Commit to a statement such as "we have the rules for a reason" or reference the family contract on technology and tell your children "family contracts are no different than legal contracts." Rest assured that if both parents stick to the plan, new habits will form and you will start to see your children become more engaged in offline activities, more social and generally happier.

Spontaneous Recovery

After the nagging to play video games or have the cellphone 24/7 subsides, you may think your children have "kicked the habit." Unfortunately, this is not always the case. There is an extensively researched concept called "spontaneous recovery" that suggests most people will eventually revert to their previous habits. This is the same concept that plagues sticking to diets and fitness routines.

For example, as part of your new family plan you purchase a program that completely blocks access to a social media site for teens and you have the program installed on the computer. Your teenager knows that you are monitoring and restricting use but may not know the specific details. This scenario is actually very likely considering the teen may storm out of the room the minute you bring up the idea and they refuse to stick around to hear the details. Now, imagine the first time your teen pulls up his or her social media account and it is rendered inaccessible. It is likely they will become angry, frustrated and try to gain access some other way, but they will eventually give up. This may also result in some angry outbursts as part of the extinction burst we discussed.

Later that night or the next day, your teen will probably try again out of habit or because they forgot about the software. You will start to notice that the attempts occur less frequently over time and if there is absolute restriction, with no access anywhere, your teen will eventually give up completely. Realistically, with social media available through other devices, there is almost no way to completely stop access. However, controlling what you can and understanding why and how spontaneous recovery is wired into us gives you an advantage to managing the behavior at home.

Looking at this process as a marathon rather than a sprint will help you conceptualize these changes as a longer journey. Remember that there are millions of other parents going through the same struggles, and by talking with others you can find support along the way.

Covert Agent: The Sneak

As you begin making changes and establishing rules, your children will attempt to use their technology secretly despite the new family policies they agreed to follow. It is not uncommon for parents to find their children awake early in the morning playing video games or asleep with their computer or cellphone. Children frequently discover where the devices are stored and will try and often succeed at taking them.

To prevent the "sneak," we recommend you have your children turn in their cellphone and gaming devices at a specific time every evening. If your teenager is worried about you invading their privacy (reading their texts or posts) simply keep the device and allow them to keep the battery (the reverse has been problematic because teens will find a way to get an extra battery). This tactic assures them that you are not looking through their private information and assures you that they are not using their devices outside of the agreed upon hours.

For computers or gaming systems, remove the power cords, turn off the Wi-Fi or have a lock on the door to the office or computer room where the devices are stored. This will prevent children from using the electronics in the middle of the night (a common occurrence when devices are accessible).

Pitting Mom Against Dad (or whoever is convenient)

When you begin implementing new rules and practices, children will try to punish one or both parents by fostering conflict between the two. This holds true when the parents are married or divorced. To combat this situation, it is crucial that both parents are on the same page concerning technology use.

Professional Help

Children who suffer significant emotional consequences from technology overuse may need professional assistance. While our book provides you with useful strategies to moderate technology use, it cannot provide your child or family with the therapy they might require. If your child has threatened to harm him or herself or demonstrated emotional variability that is difficult to control, then a therapist should be your first step. If your child appears depressed, he or she may need medication intervention coupled with therapy to normalize their mood. Any statements about self-harm or serious signs of depression are non-negotiable, urgent, and must be taken seriously.

At the Technology Wellness Center we provide a comprehensive assessment and guidance for families that include next steps to facilitate a holistic approach to technology balance. Once your child's emotions are stabilized, you can begin using some of the strategies outlined in the book, but until a child becomes emotionally healthy, these strategies may be too difficult for them to accept.

Final Word

We have covered a lot of ground in these pages and we know the information can seem overwhelming. While writing the book our objective was to provide you with valuable information and practical tools. We sought to give you guidance, help you better understand the impact of technology overuse and reassure you with tools to make the changes necessary to promote a balanced, healthy household. Our passion and commitment to proactively preventing technology overuse is rooted in our desire to help families before they find themselves facing a serious problem.

We hope that you now realize there are many children and families struggling with the same issues you might be facing in your household. After reading this book, we hope you find confidence and comfort now that you possess the knowledge and tools to proactively prevent issues from escalating. If or when challenges occur, you have strategies for managing those issues. We encourage you to be patient with yourself and your children. Focus on establishing balance with technology use and ensuring it does not hinder the necessary interpersonal connections, physical activity, emotional stability and positive behavior everyone requires to enjoy well-adjusted and successful lives.

Finally, do not be afraid to go through the assessment process on a regular basis. Remember that this is a process, one that is dynamic and constantly changing with the evolution of technology and the growth and development of our children. We suggest you revisit the TUC assessment bi-annually and build it into your health routine, much like you would a regular checkup. With the rate that kids transition through life and the speed at which new technology is released, taking the TUC every six months is ideal.

We are committed to helping parents as they go through this difficult journey and hope you will utilize the resources on our website, www. TechnologyWellnessCenter.com. We will continue to dedicate our passion and commitment to this issue and to educate, empower and support families in maintaining a balance between technology and daily life.

Acknowledgements

We would like to extend thanks to the numerous individuals who have supported us through the process of writing, editing, and finishing this book. First, Noelle Schuck, Juliet Straker, Jaime Killin, and Niamh Sutton who provided us with valuable insight during the first, second, and third edits of this book. We were lucky to have Julie Worthington graciously agree to read the book during her busy commute into the city. We especially want to thank Janet Werner and Shelby Oakes for tackling the painstaking task of crossing our t's and dotting our i's, despite their busy lives. We thank Andi Haas-Schneider for her artistic abilities and providing design suggestions for our book cover. Kathy Reisdorf and Quita Remick were instrumental in helping us develop and fine-tune our message to parents, and for that we thank them. Brian Snider and E. J. Hughes supported and guided us in the practical application of our vision. We are eternally indebted to Lieutenant Joe LeDuc, an inspiring and dedicated officer with a background in Internet crimes, who continues to provide us with his ongoing commitment to spreading our message with real life stories.

Finally, we would like to thank our husbands and children. They made numerous sacrifices so that we could write this book. They spent many days without their wives and mommies. Without their love, inspiration, and understanding this project may have never come to fruition.

About the Authors

Dr. Strohman is a licensed clinical psychologist who focuses her practice on teens and families, providing a compassionate approach to traditional therapy. Her goal is to empower her clients to work with their own strengths to find solutions to get on the right path toward wellbeing. Dr. Strohman's most notable positions have been her work as a Legislative Assistant in Congress, an Honors Intern for the FBI, and a Visiting Scholar for the FBI while collaborating to complete her dissertation. After graduation she worked at a large law firm prior to completing her residency at the Arizona State Hospital with a clinical and forensic rotation in clinical psychology. Following her residency she started consulting in business strategies working with professional athletes in wealth management and business management, setting up for-profit and nonprofit organizations across the United States. From there she returned to a full time focus in her therapy practice where she takes her wealth of experiences to meet client needs. Dr. Strohman is a member of several legal, psychological and community organizations in Arizona and nationally.

Dr. Westendorf is a licensed clinical and forensic psychologist in the state of Wisconsin. Her education in law and psychology, coupled with her experiences, allow her to have a specialized understanding of the intersection of law and mental health. Her services include criminal and civil forensic evaluations, psychological evaluations, and outpatient therapy of adults and adolescents. Her goal in therapy is to help clients identify the thoughts, feelings, and behaviors associated with their life's struggles, while empowering them to continue making changes after therapy has concluded. In addition, she spends a great deal of time testifying in court as an expert in a variety of forensic evaluations. Dr. Westendorf presents on a variety of topics involving psycholegal and ethical issues for psychologists and lawyers. Dr. Westendorf is a member of several state and national legal and psychological organizations and has served as a board member for many of those organizations. She also served as a board member of the Psychology Examining Board for the State of Wisconsin.

References

1. http://www.pewinternet.org/2012/03/19/teens-smartphones-texting/
2. http://www.cbsnews.com/news/addicted-suicide-over-everquest/
3. http://www.nytimes.com/2006/06/11/magazine/11poker.html?pagewanted=all
4. http://blog.cleveland.com/metro/2007/10/loving_child_called_a_killer.html
5. http://www.theledger.com/article/20130910/news/130919963
6. http://www.cnn.com/2015/03/01/us/suicide-text-case/
7. http://www.hup.harvard.edu/catalog.php?isbn=9780674363366
8. http://www.statista.com/statistics/232499/americans-who-use-social-networking-sites-several-times-per-day/
9. http://www.census.gov/prod/2013pubs/p20-569.pdf
10. http://www.marcprensky.com/writing/Prensky%20-%20Digital%20Natives,%20Digital%20Immigrants%20-%20Part1.pdf
11. American Psychiatric Association (2013) Diagnostic and Statistical Manual of Mental Disorders, fifth Edition, DSM-5, pg 783
12. www.ejradiology.com/article/S0720-048X(09)00589-0/fulltext
13. http://www.jneurosci.org/content/23/27/9240.full
14. http://www.ncbi.nlm.nih.gov/pubmed/17024677
15. http://www.jneurosci.org/content/23/27/9240.full
16. http://link.springer.com/article/10.1007%2FBF02138940#page-2
17. All data taken from Hagell A (2012) *Changing Adolescence: Social trends and mental health*. Bristol: Policy Press, except for those relating to numbers of 16-18 year olds in full-time education taken from DfE/BIS figures:http://www.education.gov.uk/rsgateway/DB/SFR/s000938/index.shtml
18. http://www.cdc.gov/mmwr/preview/mmwrhtml/ss6104a1.htm#Tab23
19. cdc.gov/nchs/data/hus/2013/070.pdf
20. http://www.princeton.edu/futureofchildren/publications/docs/10_02_05.pdf
21. http://kidshealth.org/parent/positive/family/tv_affects_child.html

22 A. E. Staiano, D. M. Harrington, S. T. Broyles, A. K. Gupta, & P. T. Katzmarzyk (2013). Television, Adiposity, and Cardiometabolic Risk in Children and Adolescents. American Journal of Preventive Medicine (44), pp 40-47, DOI: 10.1016/j.amepre.2012.09.049)

23 http://www.aap.org/en-us/advocacy-and-policy/aap-health-initiatives/Pages/Media-and-Children.aspx

Made in the USA
Middletown, DE
29 October 2018